Heavenly Encounters

Heavenly Encounters

EXTRAORDINARY JOURNEYS OF FAITH

Bill Vincent

ArcanaVerse Books

Contents

Copyright © 2024 by Bill Vincent

All rights reserved. No part of this book may be reproduced in any manner whatsoever without written permission except in the case of brief quotations embodied in critical articles and reviews.

First Printing, 2024

"I've transformed my sermons into book form. Please note that we've refined the content for clarity and a smoother reading experience. We trust you'll find it engaging."

1

Part One

One of the initial topics in this new ministry was God speaking about revival and various other things. I found myself wondering, 'Revival? Why talk about that?' Hallelujah! But of course, God had me talk about something I had to walk away from. People might not understand how challenging it is to be in the midst of revival and sustain it as long as I was able to in the presence of God.

God did so much during that time—hundreds of healings, miracles, signs, and wonders. It was an incredible journey. But then, at the peak of it, He told me to leave. People don't understand how difficult it is for anyone's flesh to leave. I could have just shown up at every service, declared everyone healed and set free, and gone home, guaranteed payment every time. I didn't have to work hard anymore. It got to a point where people were getting healed just by showing up. However, there were underlying issues that I didn't realize until I left, and they've been confirmed repeatedly.

It's not about a single location; God is going to move in multiple places. One of the keys to reaching there is having '3rd heaven experiences.' Some may not understand what the '3rd heaven' means, so let me explain briefly. According to the Bible, the first heaven is where we are, the second heaven is where demons and the devil operate, and the third heaven is where God reigns on His throne. Some call it the 'throne zone.' Often, we have to battle through the second heaven to access the third heaven. Multiple people in the Bible experienced the third heaven, and they shared details of their encounters. We need to believe and expect these experiences, not just for the five-fold ministry but for everyone.

In Isaiah chapter 49, verses 8-10, it speaks of a favorable time, a day of salvation, and God's help to restore the land and bring people out of darkness. This is a season of Apostolic Reformation, a re-establishment of the Church. The Church needs to regain its power and authority. We must understand that while Jesus has already won the ultimate battle, we are still called to engage in spiritual warfare. We must take hold of what God has for us with faith and expectation.

I've received numerous testimonies of God's healing and blessing recently, which reminds me that God is moving. We may not fully understand His ways, but we must humble ourselves and trust Him. Our Redeemer lives, and we should refrain from judging others until we've walked in their shoes or known the whole truth. Let's get excited about what God is doing; hunger for His presence is rising, and we're in for some amazing experiences. Praise God!

In Hebrews chapter 4, the writer emphasizes an important point in verses 8 and 9. He says, "For if Joshua had given them rest, he would not have spoken of another day after that, so there remains a Sabbath rest for the people of God." The apostle Paul was entrusted with a remarkable understanding of the Holy Spirit's strategy for leading the church. You might be wondering, "What does this have to do with third heaven experiences?" Well, let me tell you, I want a blueprint when God speaks to me about getting somewhere. I want to have a blueprint, an instruction manual, if you will. I want to understand how to get there.

All of this is leading to the fact that we are about to witness a church with power, but it won't come without third heaven experiences. That's right; that door that John saw standing open in heaven in Revelation 4, I believe it's still standing open. Nowhere in the Bible does it say it's shut. That's an open heaven! And I don't know about you, but I want an open heaven. I want to experience what Paul, John, and Elijah experienced. Biblical prophecies are pointing to what God is about to do, and we have so much to look forward to. He's pouring out His Spirit on all flesh. Get ready to see children rise up in power!

But wait, let's not rush our kids off to children's church. Maybe they should be in the crowd with us. Sure, they might get restless, but so do we sometimes. We need to reach out to the children now, while they are children, especially considering the state of the world. Even if they fidget a little, let them be here with us so God can touch them.

Many will have third heaven experiences, but let's be careful. Not everyone who claims to have them truly does. There's a lot of flakiness out there. We need to get back to the real deal. One thing we must remember is that when God pours out His glory, there are boundaries we shouldn't cross. We should never stray too far from the Bible, no matter how profound our experiences may seem.

What's in heaven? God is in heaven. So, what do we need? A revelation of God! We need to have an identity of who He is, and the Bible already provides us with all the identity we need. Reading about the experiences in heaven before I had my own helped me identify with what was happening. It's like when we say we want to prophesy, but we don't open our Bibles. To prophesy the word of the Lord, you need the word of the Lord in you. It's that simple.

When it comes to third heaven experiences, we need to remember that encountering God will change us. If you've truly been to the third heaven, you won't come back the same. Sin won't have the same hold on you. You won't return unchanged, still caught up in gossip, lying, and other sins. You'll change for the better.

In Revelation 1, we see the Lord appearing to John as a great judge. It was so overwhelming that John fell to his feet like a dead man. Can you imagine if the Lord showed up as a judge in our church on Sunday morning? We need to have a healthy fear of the Lord. But here's the thing; encountering God should leave us awestruck and changed. Let's embrace these experiences, but let's also be mindful of staying within the boundaries of God's Word.

Revival exposes hearts and brings things to the surface. People start confessing and repenting. Rocks come to the surface when the rain falls. We all want revival, but let's not just seek our preferred version of it. Let's embrace the kind of revival where repentance and transformation occur.

In today's world, we are presented with an open door to the realm of the spirit, which is truly exceptional in its excellence. This opportunity must be approached with solemn care and reverence. We have encountered experiences that demand our utmost care and reverence. I don't wish to exaggerate or say anything that isn't accurate. I prefer to maintain the purity of these experiences by not going further than necessary.

It's akin to cherishing the prophetic gift, where I am cautious about what I share. I aim to convey only the word of the Lord. Even when it comes to my encounters with God, I refrain from sharing unless it is genuinely from Him. Many people claim to see various things, but if there is no real transformation, then it raises questions.

Recently, I had an encounter with an angel, although I only saw his muscular legs during the midst of revival. His strength was remarkable, and he seemed like a formidable breakthrough angel.

I didn't see much more, but I recognized him from a previous encounter. These experiences create lasting memories, allowing us to recognize God's presence when it repeats.

This angel reappeared after over a decade, emphasizing his purpose of bringing breakthrough and rerouting the enemy. We must mature in our understanding of spiritual experiences and recognize the appropriate level of authority they grant us. Having an encounter with God doesn't automatically make us gods; it's about walking in His power and spirit.

We must be cautious not to label every experience as a "Throne room revelation" or visitation. Most of my experiences occur within the solitude of my room. While we shouldn't limit the possibility of experiencing the heavenly realms, we must avoid exaggeration and misrepresentation.

Overemphasizing or misusing spiritual experiences can lead to distortions, whether in the prophetic or giving. We should be truthful and respectful in our teachings, avoiding manipulative practices. We need to strike a balance between accountability and freedom in the body of Christ.

The gifts of the Spirit and spiritual encounters are precious treasures. Soaking in God's presence and embracing these gifts is vital, but we must avoid extremes. We are living in unprecedented times with divine opportunities before us. The mysteries of the Kingdom are unfolding, and we're on the verge of something extraordinary.

God is inviting us to come up higher. A river of glory service is in the works, where healing words of knowledge will be released. It's a time of great divine opportunities. Let's remain humble, seeking God's wisdom and guidance as we move forward.

We must humbly acknowledge that we don't know everything. I've been to numerous prophet and minister gatherings where various ministers would speak, and I would eagerly attend every service with a heart open to receive. I'd even invite fellow ministers to join me in the evening service even if they weren't scheduled to speak. Sometimes, they declined, opting for rest, but I always saw the value in sitting and receiving from others.

It's essential to recognize that no matter our position, whether as a prophet or an apostle, we all need to be willing to sit in services and receive ministry. Sometimes, pride can hinder us from learning and growing further because we believe we've already reached a certain level of maturity. I recall an apostle once claiming that he knew everything there was to know. I couldn't help but think that if that were true, he should be in heaven already. Sadly, he delivered his sermon arrogantly, claiming he could perform many miracles, but the congregation wasn't ready for them.

A prophet, who was present that day, privately prophesied to him, advising him to step down for a year due to the misuse of his authority. To our surprise, he followed this advice and took a year off. Repentance is vital in moments like these.

This divine invitation to the third heaven is not to be taken lightly. We can't simply assume it will happen whenever we desire it. Sometimes, when I've been fortunate enough to experience signs and wonders, it doesn't happen predictably in every service. I don't take it for granted. I press into the Lord with the same intensity each time, as if it were the first time. We must go after it with a fresh hunger every time.

Revival is a precious gift, and maintaining it can be challenging. We should avoid setting time limits on God's presence. We often become complacent, assuming God will always show up. We need to be aware that His timing might not align with ours, and that's perfectly fine. We must learn to treasure His presence, regardless of how or when He manifests.

God sometimes surprises us with His signs and wonders, like gemstones or gold dust. These manifestations are God's treasures, and there's plenty for everyone. We mustn't get caught up in who receives them but rather rejoice in God's generosity. Let's welcome His presence in whatever form it comes.

Sometimes, we've had experiences where signs and wonders have accompanied our worship or preaching. However, we've unintentionally become too focused on the signs themselves and allowed them to become routine. We've set strict schedules and unintentionally limited God's move. We should break free from such constraints and let God have His way.

We must approach these divine encounters with reverence and humility, acknowledging that they are not to be taken for granted. We should maintain a hunger for God's presence and not box Him into a specific time frame or method. God's ways are unpredictable, and His treasures are meant to be shared, not hoarded. Let's stay open to His surprises and maintain a heart of worship and awe.

I don't have all the answers. There are valid points on both sides of the conversation. I'm not the judge, and I thank Jesus for that. Let's all say 'amen' and praise God for His judgment because, honestly, there are times I might be too lenient or too harsh if I were the one in charge. Let's start over, God, with a fresh flood of Your grace. Any day now, I'm ready to pick up the pieces and move forward. Thank You, Lord; You are truly good.

In the midst of all the discussions and debates, as we reflect on what God has done in our midst, we must remember that He's preparing to bring a magnificent revival that the world has never seen. Despite the attempts of the enemy to distract us and divert our focus, God is about to manifest His glory in an unprecedented way.

It's crucial to understand that He has halted a move of God that could have been tainted. We need to grasp the significance of this. If we had deviated from our true purpose, we could have become hardened and unable to course-correct. We might have wasted years spinning our wheels. But God has given us a wake-up call.

He recently revealed to me that He is about to expose the

true hearts of those in this revival. He will unveil people's motives and intentions. The unveiling has already begun; can you sense it? Hearts are being exposed.

I, too, have had to repent during these past few months for the role I played in certain situations. I allowed myself to become consumed with what was happening, aligning myself with decisions I now regret. I am not claiming to be better than anyone else; I've had to repent.

After this season of reflection, God is shaping a new, leaner, and more powerful ministry. He will open doors and windows of heaven and pour out His blessings. We cannot become overly religious or rigid in our ways, for God's plans are about to shake, rattle, and roll the church. Extraordinary transformations are on the horizon.

I am grateful for what I have seen and experienced during these three months. I wouldn't trade it for the world. It's not about the gemstones or multiplied money; it's about the heart. God can restore material possessions, but the heart is where He truly operates.

Provision is always there. It might have looked different these past few months, but God's faithfulness remains unwavering. We've been reminded that faith is essential when we seemingly have nothing. We must remain thankful and ready for the explosion of blessings that awaits us.

As we prepare for the remarkable revival that God is ushering in, let us also pray for the ability to forgive those who have opposed us. Forgiveness is a powerful weapon against opposition and negativity. We are all on the same team, even if we're not under the same roof. Let us unite in love and prayer. Thank you, Lord Jesus.

2

Part Two

First of all, I want to express my gratitude for your word, Lord. We thank You for tonight, where we are going to delve into the topic of the third heaven. However, I don't want this to be merely a discussion in words; I desire that in the days ahead, we have real experiences akin to those of Paul. Like Paul, I want to be able to say, 'I don't know whether in the body or out of the body, but I know I've been with God.' I want us all to have these experiences together, Lord, in Jesus' name.

In this time, I believe we are on the verge of witnessing the greatest things we've ever seen in our lives. This week, something remarkable happened to me. At first, there was very little, but then I felt the presence of an Angel named Breakthrough. I'm grateful for that encounter. However, God has been speaking to me about third heaven experiences. He wants to take us there, and I am eager for it.

Third heaven experiences are undeniably real, and I discussed this to the best of my ability last night. Tonight, I want to focus on the warning aspect of such encounters. It's important to establish

10

boundaries when pursuing these experiences. Our boundary, which we must never cross, is the Word of God. If something is not in alignment with the Bible, we should avoid it. We should never take our experiences beyond what aligns with the Word.

Throughout history, many individuals have pushed the limits of these experiences beyond biblical principles and parameters. We must be cautious not to become like them. Our stewardship of this responsibility falls upon those who seek to explore this dimension of God's will.

Every time we encounter the Lord, there is spiritual fruit produced. These experiences should bear fruit. I had a profound experience three years ago, and it bore significant fruit, including gemstones, gold dust, signs, wonders, healings, miracles, and people being touched by the Holy Spirit. However, I don't want to live off past experiences. I want something new. I don't desire another round of the same glory. I want fresh encounters with God.

Let's not forget the boundaries when we operate in the prophetic, healing, or any ministry. Sometimes we may be tempted to replicate what worked in the past, but we must stay within the boundaries of God's Word.

In the midst of receiving letters and feedback, there are those who question signs and wonders. However, I don't need to prove signs and wonders; God Himself is the proof. We must remember that God's ways often transcend what is recorded in the Bible.

Now, let's turn to the scripture and explore Isaiah's throne room experience in Isaiah 6:1.

In the year of King Uzziah's death, I had a vision. I saw the Lord sitting on a lofty and exalted throne, and the train of His robe filled the temple. This vision, like Isaiah's response to it, is described in Isaiah 6. Isaiah said, 'Woe is me, for I am ruined! Because I am a man of unclean lips, and I live among a people of unclean lips; for my eyes have seen the King, the Lord of hosts.' Last night,

I mentioned that if everyone truly had a third heaven experience, they would undergo a transformation. You wouldn't have such experiences while carrying your baggage; God would cleanse you along the way.

I also talked about the practice of tying a rope around the priest's ankle before entering the Holy of Holies in the temple. If they had any sin or impurity in their hearts, they would die inside, and the rope would be used to pull them out. It's almost like saying some of us might need a metaphorical rope when entering the third heavens, just in case we stray. We need to recognize that if everyone was genuinely having these experiences, there would be visible fruit.

I shared a story about a woman who claimed to have gone to the third heavens during our services. Initially, I commended her, but as she continued to speak and her life did not reflect a transformation, it raised questions. She became upset over every sermon, thinking I was targeting her. When she met with us to discuss her grievances, none of them were valid. Despite her claims of heavenly experiences, her behavior and character remained unchanged. This made me question the authenticity of her experiences.

I also discussed how these experiences often begin in our imagination. It's important to focus our thoughts on God, and we must bring every thought into obedience to Christ. When we're truly pursuing God's presence, He will start refining every aspect of our lives.

I shared a personal story of pressing into God a few years ago and how it led to a season of conviction and transformation. I had to give up habits and distractions that took time away from seeking His presence. It's crucial to recognize that drawing near to God often involves sacrificing things that hinder our relationship with Him.

I mentioned a prophet who sacrificed his beloved Dr. Pepper during a period of seeking God. This act of obedience and sacrifice appeared to lead to powerful ministry results. Sometimes, our willingness to let go of things that distract us from God's presence can lead to remarkable outcomes.

I touched on Isaiah's stand against apostasy and his unwavering commitment to purity and truth, even at the cost of his life. When we take a stand for righteousness, it may come with a high personal cost, but it's essential to remain steadfast in our faith.

I want to share an important point. Sometimes people claim to have had experiences in the third heaven during corporate meetings. Just imagine all of us gathered together, receiving prophetic words about lifting the entire church into the heavens. However, we must remain discerning to ensure that these experiences are genuine and not counterfeit. We shouldn't seek hype; we should seek the authentic presence of God.

I've heard stories of individuals claiming incredible experiences, but we must be cautious about such claims. It's essential not to declare that we've had an experience until we're absolutely sure. Let's not be like those flyers advertising "powerful prophetic anointing" or "miracles, signs, and wonders" when the reality falls short.

We need to understand that when we have a genuine experience in the third heaven, it marks us profoundly. These experiences leave an indelible mark on our spirits. It's like a memory etched into our souls, driving us to seek those encounters again. However, God's ways can change, and we must remain open to His leading.

Equipping warriors is what we are called to do. When you have an experience in the third heaven, you are equipped like never before. God's arsenal of spiritual weaponry is far superior to any military technology. We must ensure that we are mature enough to handle these advanced spiritual weapons. Just as rookies in the military must undergo training before using sophisticated weapons, we too must grow and mature in our faith before being entrusted with heavenly weaponry.

God wants to give us advanced spiritual weaponry, but it requires growth and maturity. He desires warriors who can enter a household, break chains, and set people free. We need the anointing to resurrect dead churches and bring transformation wherever we go. We should aspire to be spiritual warriors, like the ultimate warrior for God, breaking strongholds and advancing His kingdom.

Let me share an incredible story about a man who went through a difficult phase in life. He ended up getting into drugs and alcohol, which eventually led to his downfall and expulsion from wrestling. He faced humiliation and many challenges. However, there's a remarkable twist to his story – he found salvation.

I saw him on TV during an interview with another wrestler who happened to have their own show. It's fascinating how wrestlers sometimes transition to television. God works in mysterious ways.

Speaking of media, we have access to various forms of mass media today, such as the Internet, television, and smartphones. These are powerful tools in our hands. Allow me to share a fantastic story about a woman who attended our revival meetings. She got so deeply touched by the presence of God that she didn't even notice the signs and wonders happening around her. She remained in that state even after the meetings ended. She took a picture and sent it to a friend in Georgia. However, her friend didn't respond. It turns out that the picture had a profound spiritual impact on her friend, and she was unable to reply. This woman's life began to change dramatically, even though she had never physically attended our meetings. This highlights the power of mass media to spread the impact of God's work.

When we experience God's presence, we can share it with others through various media. Sometimes, we tend to focus too much on the signs when the true essence is the glory of God. Signs are just indicators of His presence.

Now, let's talk about equipping. God provides equipping

ministries to develop gifts and callings. He wants us to be fully loaded with everything we need. Just like a fully loaded car with all the bells and whistles, we should aim to be spiritually fully furnished.

When we access the third heaven in the spirit, we rise above earthly problems and challenges. In this realm, we embrace hope, overcome hopelessness, and conquer fear with faith. Faith eliminates fear.

We have a responsibility to enjoy the freedom we have as the Church, especially here in America. While challenges may arise in the future, let's cherish our current freedom and make the most of it. And as for prophecies and predictions about the end times, there are various beliefs and interpretations, but we should always be ready and focused on our faith in God's plan.

Have you ever heard of Maria Woodworth-Etter? She's one of the most profoundly spiritually experienced women I've come across. Of course, I never met her in person, which would be impossible since she's no longer alive. However, we can gain valuable insights from her books and writings. Maria Woodworth-Etter was a remarkably powerful woman. Her ministry was marked by visions and revelations, which played a significant role.

She had numerous visions, and during her meetings, people would have visions of their own destinies, especially related to missionary work. It was incredible to witness as they started speaking the foreign languages of the countries they were called to. This was a clear manifestation of the supernatural.

It's essential to understand that despite her powerful ministry, Maria faced opposition. Some attendees, both sinners and saints, would ridicule and mock her during meetings. It's astonishing to think about how she remained steadfast in her ministry despite the challenges.

I want to share some details from her writings because they

highlight her determination to continue her services despite the difficult circumstances. Many individuals who were oppressed by various forms of sickness and spiritual bondage experienced supernatural encounters during her meetings. The encounters led to their deliverance and miraculous healings. It was truly a remarkable time.

In each meeting, a tangible atmosphere of revelation and encounter would envelop the room. Attendees would feel the change, even those who initially came with skepticism or mockery. This transformation touched everyone present, even those who had doubted her ministry.

In one instance, Maria Woodworth-Etter faced a particularly hostile crowd in St. Louis, MO. People stood on chairs with hats, smoking cigars and pipes, and exhibiting disrespectful behavior. However, as the meeting progressed and the presence of God became tangible, they began to change. Men removed their hats and pipes, while women covered themselves out of reverence. Some even fell as if overcome by the presence of God.

This is a testament to the impact of her ministry and the undeniable evidence of heavenly encounters. It's essential to recognize that genuine encounters with the third heaven produce lasting fruit. Maria Woodworth-Etter's ministry was marked by authenticity and purity, and we need more of that in the church today.

In conclusion, we are in a significant season where prophetic ministry is on the rise. Credible prophets and apostles are emerging, bearing pure words from heaven. We must seek the genuine encounters with the third heaven, discerning the fruit of these experiences. As we pursue these encounters with God, we can expect a fresh outpouring of revelation and the emergence of trustworthy prophetic voices in the church.

Let's embrace this season of prophetic ministry and eagerly anticipate the word of the Lord being released in our midst.

About the Author

Diving deep into the realms of spiritual awakening, Bill Vincent embodies a connection with the Supernatural that spans over three decades. With a robust prophetic anointing, he has dedicated his life to ministry, serving as a guiding light and a pillar of strength in Revival Waves of Glory Ministries.

Bill Vincent is not just a Minister but a prolific Author, contributing to the spiritual enlightenment of many through his diverse range of writings and teachings. His work encompasses themes of deliverance, fostering the presence of God, and shaping Apostolic, cutting-edge Church structure. His insights are drawn from a wellspring of experience, steeped in Revival, and fine-tuned by a profound Spiritual Sensitivity.

In his relentless pursuit of God's Presence and his commitment to sustaining Revival, Bill focuses primarily on inviting divine encounters and maintaining a spiritual atmosphere ripe for transformation. His extensive library of over 125 books serves as a beacon of hope, guiding countless individuals in overcoming the shackles of Satan and embracing the light of God.

Revival Waves of Glory Ministries is not your typical church – it's a prophetic ministry, a sanctuary where the Holy Spirit is given the freedom to move as He wills. Our sermons, a blend of divine wisdom and revelation, can be experienced on Rumble, immersing you in the transformative power of the Word: https://rumble.com/c/revivalwavesofgloryministriesbillvincent

For a deeper exploration into our teachings, visions, and the manifold grace of God, visit https://www.revivalwavesofglorymin-istries.com/.

Embark on a journey of spiritual discovery with Bill Vincent, and let the waves of revival wash over you, unveiling the divine power and boundless love of God!

Podcast: https://podcasters.spotify.com/pod/show/bill-vincent2

Rumble: https://rumble.com/c/revivalwavesofgloryministries-billvincent

Be sure to check out our new videos **Downloads From Heaven!**

www.ingramcontent.com/pod-product-compliance
Lightning Source LLC
Chambersburg PA
CBHW031257130726
47988CB00008B/3389